# CONSEN VOTING SYSTEMS

by

P.J. Emerson

# INTRODUCTION

He listened carefully to all the arguments, pondered for a moment or two, and then said,

"No, I don't like it."

"Why not?" was the obvious rejoinder.

"Because," said he, the Communist Party chairperson of the local council's executive committee in the Russian town of Kirov, "you cannot predict the results."

"SAMIZDAT"

Printed by Noel Murphy (Printing)

Typeset by the Community Computer Resource Centre,

Hazelwood Integrated College

First Published 1991

ISBN 0 9506028 3 3

No rights reserved,

for like all good ideas,

they belong to the noosphere.

By the same author:

"Northern Ireland - That Sons May Bury Their Father" 1979, ISBN 0 906676 00 2

"Consensus - Democracy without opposition" Moscow News, No 6/89

"Consensus", "Novy Mir", No 3/90

"Power, the psychology and politics of consensus", "Pravo i Vlast", Progress Publishers, Moscow, 1990, ISBN 5 01 003214 7

"Not by the majority alone", "Debaty" [Bulgaria], No 17/90

And on a different theme:

"Inflation? Try a Bicycle", the story of an 8,000 mile cycle ride in Central Africa, 1978, ISBN 0 9506028 0 9

"The Dove of peace a'learning how to fly", some poetry from a peace camp, ISBN 0 9506028 1 7

"What an extraordinary Title for a Travel Book", a comparison of western European and African eco-systems, 1986, ISBN 0 9506028 2 5

# DEDICATION

No ideas belong to only one person, and for everything in the pages which follow, my thanks must first go to the noosphere in general, for It has done unprompted wonders, and then to Dervla Murphy in particular, for she it was who encouraged me to tackle this issue of consensus, twelve long years ago. The word, I think you'll agree, was not then in vogue.

I'd also like to thank the members of the New Ireland Group who, though not without some doubts, joined in a little experiment. Thus, at a 1986 public meeting in Belfast, over two hundred and fifty people discussed the constitutional future of Northern Ireland. Nearly all political parties and organisations were involved; those of the cloth met those of the gun; for the first time since the signing of the Anglo-Irish agreement, certain members of the Official Unionists sat in the same room with others of Sinn Fein; and together we found some common ground.

To any who might be a little sceptical of consensus voting systems, therefore, may I suggest that if the latter can be used successfully in Belfast, then maybe they can be deployed anywhere.

Lastly, I'd like to thank those with whom I have scrutinised this theme and conducted other experiments in Eastern and Central Europe. How warm were so many to these new ideas, how numerous the editors and journalists who then devoted their columns to this subject... and how strange that some of their counterparts in the western *news* media should persist in their support of the *old* "for-or-against".

# NOTA BENE

a) In describing any electoral system, one must from time to time resort to the language of numbers.   But since the joys of mathematics are attractive only to a few, I've confined any additional complications to the appendices.

b) I've deliberately kept the use of practical examples to a minimum, preferring to use theoretical ones where necessary, and most of those are also in the appendices.   As a practical guide to consensus, therefore, the book may be useful to all and sundry, no matter where their country or what their interests.

c) I've also refrained from giving you any detailed attack either of the majority vote system or of PR-STV (Proportional Representation - Single Transferable Vote).   The latter is a mighty improvement on the former, but even it is subject to many imperfections, of which I'll mention just the one (see page 29).

In this little pamphlet, then, I'll only sing the praises of consensus. I criticise not another's point of view; I merely advocate my own.

# HEAR HEAR, THERE THERE

Glory to God in the Highest
And on Earth to the one-party state;
The angels sing ho-ho-hosannah
*While the masses fulfil the decisions of the eighty-third plenum of the*
*presidium of the politbureau of the communist party of the Union of Soviet*
*Socialist Republics...*
And there ain't much old ho-ho in that.

Glory to God in the pulpit
And on earth to the two-party state
Whose members vote for for-or-against:
*"This house believes that the unanimous vote of the one-party state is a*
*blatant infringement of the people's democratic and God-given right, to have*
*hold and hate an opponent,"*
And both whips crack hip hip hoorah!

Glory to God in the lowest
And on Earth to the one who shall state:
"In future just so-so societies,
Politicians will not talk so much."
Whence we'll all say, "Good God. You're right."

# CONTENTS

# FOREWORD

When they stop to think about it, it becomes clear to all moderately intelligent human beings that consensus politics is the way forward - the only way forward. Unfortunately most people don't stop to think about such matters. They accept our present form of pseudo-democracy like they accept the weather; it often does nasty things - is inconvenient, even hazardous - but there's nothing anyone can do about it. This of course is partially true;  there's nothing any individual can do to change our political systems. But if enough individuals do stop to think about it, and form groups to demonstrate that consensus politics can work, and that the majority of the population want this new system, then something would  - eventually - happen.

The snag is that tiny groups, scattered here and there, won't ever rock the pseudo-democratic boat.  It is well defended; it has a lot of Fat Cats on board who would quickly become slimmer if consensus politics took off. So mass conversions are needed - and soon, before the myopic Fat Cats inadvertently write  FINIS  to the story of mankind.

Peter Emerson's brilliant new book, if sufficiently widely read, could considerably speed up the conversion process.  It proves that pseudo-democracy  is not only obsolete but perilous to the highest degree.  And it clearly explains how consensus politics operates.  The notion is not just more fall-out from the latest explosion of utopian ideals.  It's a practical way of running humanity's affairs and has been used, in some societies, for centuries.  It really is workable, if enough people want to make it work.

Read Consensus Voting Systems and encourage everyone you know to read it - and to discuss it and think of ways in which its message might be applied within their own sphere of action.  Make people realise that this is not merely another fad, that if we had not been so successfully zombified by our inherited political environment, our instinct for self-preservation would have us all out on the streets NOW, insisting on consensus politics.

*Dervla Murphy*

# DEFINITIONS

## Preferendum

The *"preferendum"* is a linear multiple-choice voting procedure in which

(a)   there shall always be at least 3, usually from 6 to 10, and seldom more than 12, candidates or options; and

(b)   the voter shall, in his/her own order of choice, cast his/her preference points *for all* the candidates or options listed.

## Matrix Vote

The *"matrix vote"* is a tabular multiple-choice voting procedure in which the voter may not only choose those whom he/she wishes to be his/her representatives, but also state in which posts he/she wishes them to serve.

## Consensus

The *"general consensus"* on any one issue is that which is perceived to be the agreed opinion of an overwhelming number, though there may be some who dissent.

A decision taken *"in consensus"* is one reached without resort to a "for-or-against" vote; instead, those concerned either come to a verbal agreement with which none of the participants now dissent; or they vote thereon by using a consensus voting system, and find that which, collectively speaking, enjoys a *"level of consensual support"* of, let us say, 75% or more.

A *"level of consensus"* is the perceived or calculated level with which those concerned support a particular candidature or proposal.

100% consensus for any one candidate or policy option infers that all agree unanimously either that that candidate should be elected, or that that policy should be adopted; it does not suggest there are no differences of opinion viz-a-viz the other candidates/options, nor even unanimity of mind on the chosen candidate or proposal.

A *"consensual democracy"* is one in which

(a),    all elections shall be conducted under a consensus voting system; and

(b),    both the electorate in general preferenda, and their chosen representatives in chamber, shall take all (non-emergency) decisions in consensus.

# PREFACE TO THE PREFERENDUM

## Challenge to Centralism

In the late 1960's and early '70's, people began to feel that the cause of so much social unease had little to do with arguments right-v-left, church-v-state, capitalism-v-communism, but rather to the relentless movement of power and control away from the citizen in community and towards remote centralised institutions. Active participation, where it existed at all, provided merely the appearance of democracy without any real substance. Even those with rising standards of living began to realise just how powerless they were when it came to an effective input into decision-making.

In 1968 and quite out of the blue, the French students rose up and gave a lead to the youth of Europe; it *almost* became an historical watershed. They challenged all forms of bureaucratic centralism, but they seemed to be somewhat uncertain about how to replace that which they were attempting to brush aside. Even so, at radical meetings everywhere in the years which followed, concepts of consensus democracy, institutional politics and community development became the common currency.

Around the same time, intellectual dissidents in Central and Eastern Europe were striving through a network of *samizdat* to undermine the central control of the Soviet Empire. And in the Western World, a vocal objection was mounted against the remote controlling forces of multi-national capital; it was not possible, however, to target so effectively the latter's commanding heights", for while those at the controls were accountable to their major shareholders, they seemed to remain as distant as ever to those who worked for them.

**Right to Self-Determination**
In Africa and elsewhere, long before the French students hammered at the ramparts of institutional imperialism, the struggle for independence had been developing its own momentum, and the promulgation of the right to self-determination had been a central factor therein. By reference to this right, first asserted in the Atlantic Charter of 1944, various indigenous majorities acquired a tool with which to rid themselves of minority colonial rule. But their frontiers, earlier imposed by conquest and often maintained by force, seldom - if ever - contained a homogenous, ethnic, sectarian, linguistic people. And it soon became apparent that the replacement of the old regime by majority rule could be just as unacceptable to the new minorities as had been their earlier lot.

The right to self-determination was - and still is - a catch-cry in urgent need of qualification... especially if it's intended to be part of the much vaunted New World Order. Regrettably, many new administrations have used such majoritarianism as if it was the key stone of democracy, yet this it most certainly is not. Democracy can be described as "taking the people into partnership". Thus the right to self-determination can only claim to be a fundamental right if it is clearly rooted in the consensus of the people.

While we might consider the significance of this right as it affects Greeks and Turks in Cyprus, Shona and Matabele in Zimbabwe, Tamils and Ceylonese in Sri Lanka, Hungarians and Romanians in Transylvania, Armenians and Azeris in Nagorny-Karabakh, and so on, an example nearer home is worth highlighting. In Ireland, Irish Republicans affirm the right of the people of Ireland to self-determination, and Northern Loyalists do the same for the people of Northern Ireland. Thus this fundamental human right, as enshrined in the UN Covenants on Human Rights, contains the potential for conflict rather than for its resolution.

Hence that which has been described as the politics of Chinese boxes, of peoples who are a minority in one context and a majority in another.

If the right to self-determination is to be a legitimate expression of democracy, it must be qualified by the need to achieve a consensus for same. This, of course, demands that we explain both the term itself, and the means by which it can be achieved and assessed. It is in this last regard that the Preferendum as invented by the author is such an important contribution to the evolution of democratic politics.

## Powerlessness and Consensus

In the final analysis, consensus is a condition in which there is free, overall acceptance of the manner in which power has been distributed. Thus consensus is as much to do with well-being at local community and district level as it is about the more abstract appreciation at regional and national levels. If consensus is to be central to our political *modus operandi*, it must be felt where we live and work, not merely seen as something which we strive to produce in a national parliament.

In addition to our differences ethnic, religious and linguistic, there are those of ideology, understanding, awareness, status, and so on. Differences occur naturally, and a recognition thereof is vital for the building of a consensual framework. Uniformity, on the other hand, is something so unnatural that it has to be imposed. In this respect it is worth recalling that one of the primary eco-principles affirms that the more complex and diverse the eco-system, the more stable it is. Variety is indeed the spice of life, and the more ways we have of looking at a problem, the less likely will any one way dominate exclusively, and the more likely will we successfully canvass support for the average. In using the Preferendum, we endeavour to find that option which can claim the greatest degree of consensus.

## Difference and Democracy

Unity will only be built by acknowledging that which is natural: the right to be different and our need for each other. Majoritarianism is a recipe for domination rather than a democratic system. Consensus on the other hand encourages the concept of partnership which is central to democracy. The Preferendum and Matrix Vote are significant contributions to an era which promises freedom yet risks chaos, for they recognise that "all men and women are unique and different, yet all are part of the same humanity".

The author of this contribution to the politics of tomorrow has had wide experience as a community worker locally as well as a new world thinker in many different countries and situations. It is through Peter Emerson that new democratic ideas generated in Belfast have been published in a number of journals in Central Europe and the Soviet Union. When he took off on his bicycle to Moscow some years ago, none of us who knew him well were the least bit surprised!

John Robb
*Ballymoney*
*22.8.91*

# CHAPTER 1

# THE SPIRIT OF CONSENSUS

When we come together in the spirit of consensus, we come to talk *with* each other, and to resolve any problems we may have *with* each other. Each may make his/her positive contribution; but an essential feature of consensus politics is that no-one need negate the views of another.

In those democratic forums wherein consensus is not the norm, people first talk *with* each other but then, on taking a decision, they vote (for or) *against*. Therein, the system fails. In consensus politics, however, we may talk and we may vote, but we neither talk nor vote *against*.

Consensus has been a vital part of many human relationships for years and years, of course. It is, or should be, a part of every home. And it ought to be a part of every gathering, be it on the streets, at work or at play. No-one should insist on only his/her own point of view; each should be able to participate; and all should accept the final agreement.

Alas, as we know, such is rarely seen in parliaments and councils. When power is the prize, those involved tend to split into two and both sides then struggle to win that power, fighting each other with words, or worse, and joining together in consensus only when fighting a war abroad.

War, however, must be regarded as an *irrational* form of behaviour. Political leaders resort thereto when they feel all *rational* attempts at resolving the particular dispute have failed. After that, it's win or lose, no compromise, victory or defeat, winner takes all and loser gets nought.

But it's exactly these phrases which also define our so-called democracy: people resort to a vote if all else has failed; thereafter, it's for-

or-against, no third opinions, and the stronger side takes all to then dominate the weaker.

Not only does the theatre of war resemble the political scene, so too do the two sets of actors. Both generals and politicians take sides, and each then talks of the mutual exclusivity of his or her case, so suggesting that the other side's opinion is a diametric opposite. In so doing, they rule out any compromise. And that, might I suggest, is also an irrational act.

What's more - and this is definitely a sign of irrational behaviour - if someone else comes along to present a third opinion, the two combatants may well join in a combined opposition thereto. The logic is easy enough: each side claims it is right and the other is wrong, so the very existence of a third point of view might suggest and even prove that both were mistaken.

Sometimes, of course, a third opinion is more to one side than the other. In which case, the other is delighted by that which appears as a split in the former's ranks. Indeed, he might actually encourage same, befriending this new political opposite to thus weaken the original one. As in war, so too in politics, an enemy's enemy is a friend, and this also leads to irrational conduct. Such was the case in 1933 when the German Communists refused to co-operate with their political neighbours, the Socialists, and thus they helped their opposites, the fascists, come to power. It was all a result of dogmatism, of certain individuals insisting that only they were right, of these and their supporters always thinking in terms of two supposedly mutually exclusive opposites.

Such irrational behaviour is alas the norm; but it need not, and it need never be so!

Let me take just two examples, one local, the second global.

There are many who say that Northern Ireland must be *either* a part of the United Kingdom, *or* a part of a United Ireland, inferring if not stating that the first proposal mutually excludes the second. Yet would it not be better to put the question in a different way, like this: a 6- or 9-county Northern Ireland could be administered by, devolved within, federated with, independent of, or integrated into (the nations of) Britain and/or (the Provinces of) Ireland. That's at least ten proposals already, and not one of them mutually excludes all the other nine. There's much in common, for instance, between a UK-type devolution and a UI-type federation, and it's called a semi-autonomous Northern Ireland!

In any true democracy, the people and/or their representatives would be allowed to express their views, not just on two diametric opposites, but on all the other options as well; whence one of them would almost certainly be seen as a most sensible compromise.

Alas, such is not to be, yet. The Northern Ireland problem persists, and largely because of a belief in majoritarianism, a belief which is neither rational nor justifiable, but a belief which nevertheless dominates nearly all national parliaments, be they of the old one-party states or be they of the so-called democracies.

My second example concerns an argument which very nearly led to the annihilation of all life on this planet: communism versus capitalism. The two were seen as mutually exclusive but to-day, in both camps, most say the best option is a mixed economy. Any mutual exclusivity, therefore, was totally artificial, the rantings of Reagan and Brezhnev, empty but dangerous rhetoric.

Those questions - are you British or Irish? communist or capitalist? - should never have been posed in that form. To do so was and is an irrational act, for such infer that differences there may be but of similarities there are none. Which is manifestly untrue. Likewise, in the home, one partner should never ask the other, "Will you do the washing up or won't you?" As if there could be no compromise. Indeed, in such a case, the question itself would suggest that that which had been a normal rational relationship had already broken down.

A more rational approach would consider the similarities too. Thus could be found the common ground or, to put it another way, the average public opinion; and just as, among any group of folk, there'll always be an average height, for example, so too, on any subject under the sun, there'll always be an average public opinion.

Take anything you like - arranged marriages, capital punishment, mixed education - public opinion thereon has changed with the passing of the centuries. Accordingly, on any particular subject, there existed at any one time a certain average opinion, and there now exists another. The historian claims to be able to estimate what it was; any contemporary observer should be able to calculate what it is, and with a much greater degree of accuracy. Furthermore, in any true democracy, this latter process should be central to every issue.

Now we cannot calculate the average height of a group of people by asking them only a two-option question: are you small or tall? Similarly, we cannot estimate an average opinion, simply by asking a two-option, for-or-against type question. It's mathematically impossible, especially if the answer has to be either one or the other, small or tall. The conclusion is as stark as it is simple: the for-or-against vote is actually somewhat undemocratic, and a more accurate measure is required.

The task sounds formidable enough: we must devise a more rational form of human interaction; we must allow all who wish to participate; and on whatever topic is in question, we must then estimate, as best we may, our average opinion, collective will or common consensus.

It can be found in one of two ways: either by talking and talking until eventually an agreement is reached; or by talking... and then voting, in a consensual ballot.

In the former scenario, success will only ever be achieved if all concerned first accept the need to co-operate with each other. When proceedings commence, certain proposals may already be on the table. As the debate gets under way, new suggestions will be aired, and maybe, if the level of debate is high, one good idea will lead to another. Eventually - and the whole business may often take rather a long time - a composite and compromise resolution will get maximum support: 100% consensus. Some, no doubt, will be delighted with the outcome; a few might feel it's only a step in the right direction; others would describe it as a tolerable result in the circumstances. But all agree to accept it.

Such unanimity of mind, we know, is rarely seen in any political forum. So whenever the passions are high, the subject matter controversial, the attractions of power too great, or simply the level of debate very sophisticated, the above procedures won't work; we must therefore deploy the second approach: talk and then vote.

Again, all participants must first accept the need for a certain amount of co-operation. (And just as the majoritarian democrat rejects the use of violence and agrees to abide by the final for-or-against vote, so too in consensus politics, all are obliged to reject both the force of arms and the force of numbers.)

Accordingly, and as an absolute minimum, everything must be done to ensure that the debate remains a rational multi-option discussion and doesn't descend into an irrational two-option argument. This can be achieved quite easily by stating, right at the very beginning, that at the very end, the decision will be subject not to an irrational two-option vote, but to a rational multi-option consensus poll instead. In any rational conversation, many will be the points of view; and in any rational decision-making process, many will be the options.

If everyone then expresses their opinions on all of them, thus giving an accurate expression of their particular points of view, we will be able to ascertain which suggestions are felt to be divisive, which are seen as very bad ideas, and which are regarded as rather sensible.   As in the calculation of any average, the more who participate, the better, no matter how tall or small their views.   Furthermore, in expressing a viewpoint, each shall affect the average, i.e., each shall make a contribution. And even in such conflict situations as sadly still exist in Northern Ireland, it should be possible to achieve a result which enjoys, not 100% consensus, mind, but a "level of consensus" of, say, 75%.   Indeed, as we shall see, we need never go for less.

If, in debate, everybody is aware that all suggestions will be considered, (all, that is, which do not infringe the United Nations declaration on human rights), then may a better atmosphere prevail.   Furthermore, if the decision is not to depend on the stronger of the two sides, there needn't be any, and everyone may enjoy a balanced "polylogue".

It all depends on the end; let us now, therefore, look first at how the vote proceeds, and only then shall we return to examine further the nature of the debate.

# CHAPTER 2

# THE VOTE

In consensus voting, then, I never vote against; instead, I vote for, and only for, but for all the options listed... in my own order of preference, of course.

Thus, in a ten-option "preferendum" as it is called, (an example of which is given in appendix 1), I give 10 points to the option I like the most, 9 to my next favourite, 8 to my third choice, and so on, to the end, and that includes 1 point for the option I like least of all.

In other words, I express my point of view on all of them; and in so doing, I recognise the validity of other persons' opinions. No longer do I vote *against* you, thereby hoping to outnumber and then dominate you. Rather, I join with you in the knowledge that my and your and everybody else's opinions will all influence the average and to an equal extent. I have my aspirations, and you yours; let each and everyone of us give full vent to our opinions or, to put it another way, an accurate measure thereof; and let us all then seek our common ground or collective wisdom.

Now in a two-option referendum, folks are able to vote in just one of two ways, for or against, A or B. In a three-option preferendum, however, there are six possibilities: ABC, ACB, BAC, BCA, CAB and CBA. Similarly, in a four-option ballot, there are twenty-four different ways of voting, and it all proceeds by happy mathematical progression until, in a ten-option poll, over three million different opinions or emphases may be expressed; (please see appendix 6).

If we measured all our heights to the nearest centimetre, we'd each have over two hundred different heights to choose from, and that should be good enough. Political opinions are obviously a lot more complicated, but a range of three million viewpoints should be sufficient... especially in Northern Ireland where we only have as many opinions as we have people, a mere million or so.

This may all sound a little complicated. It is. May I just point out, however, that there is a danger in simplicity, and such can be seen in the simple slogans of war! Secondly, we were all born different, and any political system which tries to negate these individual differences may be both unnatural and irrational. Thirdly, such a ten-option vote is no more complicated than a pools coupon or a UB40. And lastly, it allows and encourages everyone to think, a form of human activity not often seen in some debating chambers.

In consensus voting, then, each uses the language of numbers to express his/her point of view on all the options listed. When talking and talking, it's often the louder and more masculine who speak the most; in voting, however, all may exercise an equal influence on the final outcome which, for the moment at least, shall remain unknown. First comes the count.

# CHAPTER 3

# THE COUNT

The calculations involved are really quite easy: we add up all the points cast for each option, and express each total as a percentage of the maximum possible score, so to obtain (in this particular example) ten "levels of consensus".

That's it.

More maths, the theory of it all, you'll find in appendix 3. And less you'll find in practice, because all these sums will be done on a computer.

# CHAPTER 4

# THE ANALYSIS

The "consensors", of whom more anon, must now consider these ten consensus levels and thus ascertain the final result.

Let's assume there are 100 voters, and each casts a valid vote. If exactly 50 of these voters give their 10 points to a certain option A, if no-one gives it any 9s, 8s, or 7s, or... and if all remaining 50 give it only 1 point, then such an option will get 500 + 50 = 550 points, or a level of consensus of 55%. In consensus politics, such mean scores don't add up to much, and thus will this option A fail.

It wouldn't have helped much, either, if the figures had differed but little: if (a "majority" of) 51 had given it 10 points and 49 their 1s, it would then have got a total of 559 points or a 55.9% level of consensus. That, too, would not have been enough.

Such an option we can describe in three different ways: in diagrammatical form, it looks like this:

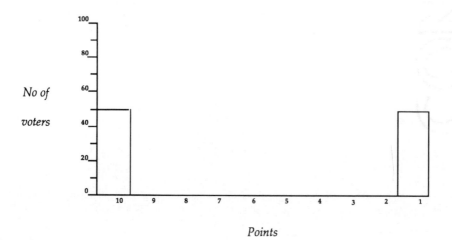

*Points*

in mathematical terms, as we've already said, it has a level of consensus of only 55%; and in words, well, it is obviously extreme, divisive and aconsensual. On all three descriptions, therefore, option A is seen to lack any genuine consensual support.

If, on the other hand, many (let's say 40) give a different option B their 10s, several (30) give it their 9s, some (20) their 8s, a few (10) their 7s, and nobody gives it anything less, then B is probably much more successful. We would paint it like this:

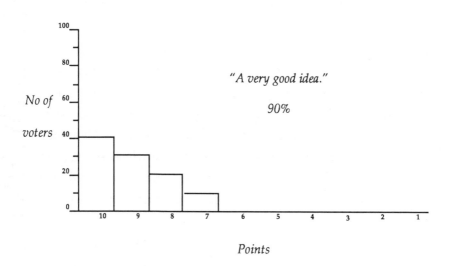

*Points*

mathematically speaking, we might add that it enjoys a

$$\frac{(40\times10 + 30\times9 + 20\times8 + 10\times7) \times 100}{1000}$$

$$= \frac{(400 + 270 + 160 + 70) \times 100}{1000}$$

$$= \frac{900 \times 100}{1000}$$

$$= \quad 90\% \text{ level of consensus;}$$

and verbally, we could say it's an excellent suggestion.    Actually, I'm rather tempted to quote myself (see page 5) and describe this result by saying that some are "delighted" with it, a few "feel it's a step in the right direction" and others that "it's a tolerable result in the circumstances". (And in fact, the above diagrammatical and mathematical descriptions may well be a much better representation of that which was spoken of earlier as getting "maximum support" or 100% consensus; so resorting to a consensus vote may mean the entire democratic process can be completed that much more accurately, and quickly!)

For a comprehensive analysis, it may be advisable to draw all ten diagrams, and basically they fall into five categories.    Something like the above "90 per-center", a curve falling from left to right, could be called *"a very good idea ";* and the higher the starting point and the steeper the curve, the greater the level of consensus.    Others are as follows:

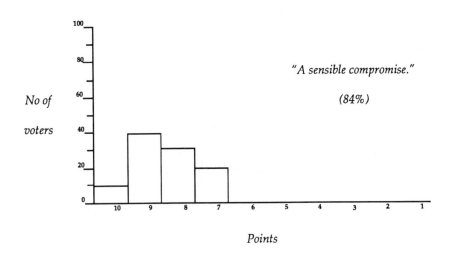

*No of*

*voters*

*"A sensible compromise."*

*(84%)*

*Points*

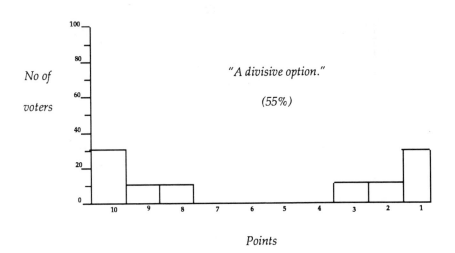

*No of*

*voters*

*"A divisive option."*

*(55%)*

*Points*

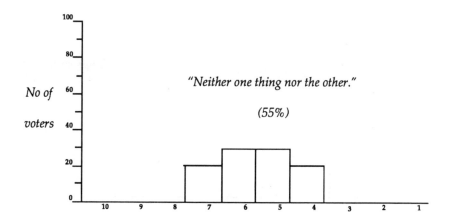

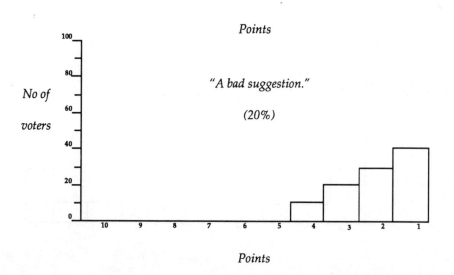

Such a comprehensive analysis can certainly do no harm; at least it will show us more clearly how we all think.

The next task is to decide which, in this case of the ten options, actually represents the average or common consensus.

Now in domestic, industrial or political conflicts, it's always best to rely on at least one impartial referee. If we left it all to a dictator, there'd be no choice at all; if we leave it to the party leaders of the two main parties, there'll rarely be a compromise; so for a rational approach to any political dispute, we need some independent and non-voting "consensors", if but to ensure that third and other opinions also get a hearing.

Accordingly, any parliamentary forum should first elect, needless to say in a preferendum, a team of say three members of the judiciary to be its consensors. In any debate, their job is threefold: to decide which proposals comply with the UN declaration and which of these best represent the debate; secondly, to choose the consensual voting system with which the matter may be resolved; and finally, to adjudicate on the result of that vote.

If one option gets a very high level of consensus, 85% or so, it must *ipso facto* be way out in front, so it may then be deemed the answer.

If, however, the subject is more controversial, maybe no one option gets such a high total and instead, two or three options get roughly equal levels of 65% or thereabouts. If so be it, the consensors will first take the most consensually popular option to be "the winner"; next they'll examine any other consensually popular options to see which parts thereof compliment this winner; and then they'll draw up a composite policy to thus make a coherent amalgam.

Politics, after all, is the art of compromise; consensus voting is simply its science.

The answer, do I hear you cry, will be too messy? Well, in similar vein, would you thus describe a mixed economy? And how would you describe a most unconsensual decision, like the 1920 Government of Ireland Act, with all its tragic and bloody consequences?

No, in principle, there' s absolutely nothing wrong with compositing; and perhaps, everything right.

Let' s think mathematically again. If the task is still to calculate that average height, we first ask all to submit an exact measure of themselves, and I think we decided the nearest centimetre will do. You're lm 73 perhaps, I'm lm 58, a third lm 62, and so it goes on, thousands of different measurements; we just bung all this info into a computer, and out comes an answer: 1 metre, 64.385 centimetres, precisely. Compositing is simply a necessary part of any accurate average estimation.

Let us therefore take a second look at the principles of analysis in a little more detail, and this time I'll choose the recent British controversy over what, if anything, was to replace the rates.

Now a good debate there would never be, if everything was seen in terms of "poll tax or the old system?" Alas, that's exactly what happened, so third and other opinions rarely got a decent hearing. If consensus had been the norm, though, all the little subtleties and nuances of different policies could have been discussed, and voted on, in a rational and civilised way. The corresponding ballot paper could well have contained the following six options:

A   The old rates system.
B   A poll tax or community charge.
C   A local income tax.
D   Local council discretion.
E   Site value rating system.
F   Property Tax.

If option D, for example, local government control, had got a very high level of consensus, local control it would have been; if it'd got a low level, central government control would have been required; and if the level had been rather average, any local control could have been subject to certain central government ceilings. The two forms of control are not mutually exclusive; and compositing, if required, may not only be possible, but desirable.

Secondly, if both option C, local income tax, and option E, site-value rating, had got roughly the same high levels of support, any future rates could have been determined both by the residents' incomes and by the value of their site.

And so on. Rarely should any one option have been seen as mutually exclusive of another. The result would doubtless have been a composite policy consisting of those options which had received good levels of consensual support; and even on such a seemingly divisive topic, this sort of combination could well have enjoyed a level of consensus of 75% or more.

Perhaps I should add at this stage that which may well be obvious: the greater the choice, the more likely will be found a near exact average and therefore a successful common consensus.

If there are but three options, two of them might be extremes, and the remaining one a very poor compromise; in which case, results will be confusing.

If, however, there are between six and ten options, some may be divisive, others extreme, a few rather weak, but one at least will come to be seen as "a most sensible compromise."

Two theoretical examples of how folks might vote, and of how such voting patterns might then be interpreted, are given in appendix 4.

# CHAPTER 5

# THE DEBATE

We now know how the debate will end: all will agree on matters uncontroversial, while on any contentious issues, they'll resort to a consensus vote.

So how should the discussions begin? Initially, no doubt, there'll be a number of motions before the house, or certain specific items on the agenda. In either case, the consensors should draw up a list of points to be considered, if but from a simple study of the subject and a cursory glance at any theoretical compromise options. Thus, to return to our example of the constitutional future of Northern Ireland, the consensors would draw up a list of about ten options, such as are listed in appendix 1, with perhaps re-partition and UN arbitration thrown in as two further items worthy of consideration.

As the debate proceeds, one or two points may be agreed upon, a few dismissed unanimously, most hotly contested; furthermore, other factors may be raised, new suggestions made, and so on.

Accordingly, the consensors will initiate, maintain, and gradually finalise a list of all disputed points, so to form a preferendum of distinct policy options. In so doing, they must ensure that all these options are as it were evenly "balanced". In the Northern Ireland case, this means that some options should reflect a British dimension, others an Irish one, a few both perhaps, and maybe one or two neither. It all depends on the debate.

Thus, even in preparing a preferendum, a certain amount of compositing may be unavoidable... or again desirable.

Consensus can be further promoted by a few simple techniques, many of which are slowly becoming more popular.

All should sit in a circle, tiered if necessary, and on convening, a moment's silence should be observed.

"Traffic lights" should be used, so to limit each verbal contribution to a certain maximum, so to ensure that everyone gets a fair share.

A second light, shaped in the form of a question mark, should be at the disposal of the consensors. Then, if someone says something which could be construed as insulting and/or inaccurate, the consensors may use this light to thus "question" these remarks. In this way, all concerned will know the point has been covered; the noise has been challenged by a light; and there'll be no need for anyone to shout.

If at any time a session does get a bit out of hand, another few moments' silence may be called for. If the rumpus continues, the rest in silence may stand and join hands, so to share their common humanity with all who wish. And if the disturbance still persists, then maybe 'tis best to adjourn. Albeit limited experience suggests, however, that such measures will rarely if ever be necessary.

Given, what's more, that all reasonable proposals will be included into the final preferendum, few should have cause to complain.

And finally... well, let's look at it this way. As we saw in the analyses, the result will be determined by an accurate measure of all opinions. So if someone wants a certain policy to be adopted, he or she must persuade not only the mild supporter to become more committed, so to give 9 or 10 points instead of just 6 or 7, but also the opponent to warm a little, now to give 6 or 7 instead of just 1 or 2. Thus there is more to be gained, not in preaching to the converted, but in gently wooing those who, in a majoritarian milieu, would have been seen as political adversaries.

Furthermore, the proponent of any one policy will have a vested interest in its non-exclusivity, and he or she will wish to show how it could enhance, or be enhanced by, some or all of the other options.

Thus the very use of a consensual system will in itself promote consensus, both in the course of a civilised debate, and in any resolutions which may follow.

# CHAPTER 6

# ELECTIONS

Whether we're choosing policies or people, be it in chamber or in the country at large, the same spirit of consensus should apply.

So again, nobody votes against his/her fellow human beings. Rather, we cast our preferences *for all* candidates listed, thereby recognising the candidature of each. In other words, we vote for everyone, regardless of their age, sex, colour, religious belief or... well, read on.

In any one set of consensus elections, we always vote for at least two persons, both the chairperson and a vice-chair, for example. Accordingly, as before, there shall always be at least three candidates, usually rather more.

Consensus voting can be used on all the following occasions: -

A)   when we the *electors*  are choosing  (i) our representatives, and/or
                                                                  (ii) our executive; or

B)   when they the *elected*  are choosing  (i) their representatives or
                                                                  executive, and/or
                                                                  (ii) a sub-committee.

### A(i)  Choosing our Representatives

In both local and general elections, the country shall be divided up into multi-member constituencies, each to send from three to six councillors or parliamentarians to the relevant forum.  In this respect, so far, it's all rather similar to PR-STV.

If the number of candidates is twelve or less, the corresponding ballot paper shall be similar to the preferendum shown in appendix 1.   All named candidates shall be allowed to describe themselves and/or their party affiliations in a limited number of words; and the instructions will differ but slightly from those shown in the appendix; (again, I choose the example of a ten-candidate ballot).

*"Write a 10 opposite the candidate whose policies you like the most; write a 9 opposite the candidate whose policies you like second best... " and so on.*

In a three-seater constituency, the three candidates with the three highest levels of consensus will then be deemed elected.

In the event of a tie, the candidate with the greater number of 10s (to stick to our current example) will be the successful one; if they're still neck-and-neck, we'll look at their 9s' totals, and so on.

And if one of the chosen few then dies or whatever, the consensors will just refer back to the preferendum results and choose the next most popular candidate; (bye-elections are only a part of an obsolescent system in which those who held or aspired to power seldom sought a compromise).

When there are more than twelve candidates, the above procedure may be a little impracticable. In such circumstances, it's therefore better to hold two rounds: in the first, each voter shall choose, in his/her order of preference, just six candidates, giving 6 points to his/her favourite, 5 to his/her next preference, etc.. Whence we add up all the points cast for each candidate and select the ten most popular ones. These then enter a second round ballot and in this, as in the above ten-candidate preferendum, each shall vote for all.

It must be emphasised that we would never wish to see a second round in which only two participated; such, alas, is our present system, if we're French or Russian, for example. If there were twenty candidates in the first encounter, then let there be a full ten in the second, for that will allow for a fair degree of proportionality (or compromise) in the results.

Elections consisting of two rounds, however, will probably, be a rarity; folks, after all, tend to tire of too many treks to the polling stations. Indeed, in a really consensual democracy such as we'll consider in the next chapter, two-tier polls need never occur.

### A(ii) Choosing our Executive

If our parliaments so decide, we the constituents may have one set of elections for the legislature, and another for the executive; indeed, if we're Americans, that's exactly what we've got.

As suggested above, however, we should never vote for but one person; as an absolute minimum, therefore, we should be electing both a president and his/her vice, and it would be better still if we were able to choose yet other members of the president's council at the same time. So, to stick to the USA for the moment, if Bush is the most consensually popular candidate, he will duly be president; but if, in the same elections, Jackson is the second most popular, then he will move into the White House as well. The two must then work together, just as their multi-racial electorate must live together... and to this theme we shall return.

### B(i) Choosing their Executive

We, the electors, choose a parliament; and parliament, if it so wishes, may then "choose" its executive or government. Such is our unhappy majoritarian lot, if we're British or Irish, for example.

First of all, though, if you'll excuse me, I'll digress. The for-or-against vote and the x-vote are, in effect, point decisions. We have a choice of perhaps only two alternatives, and each voter is required to opt for just one of them. It is, therefore, a very limited decision making process, and a very primitive one too.

In PR-STV perhaps, and in the preferendum definitely, we progress from a point decision to a line of information. And as we saw on page 7 and/or appendix 6, the corresponding degree of choice is that much greater.

A further logical step is to move to the second dimension, the page; and when any elected body chooses its executive, the better method is this, the so-called matrix vote. Here it is.

For the sake of simplicity, let us assume that all concerned have decided, in consensus, to elect a government consisting of only six ministers: a premier, a deputy, and four ministers of peace, health, tax and land. Each member may then choose, in his/her order of preference, six names, each to serve in one particular post. The relevant ballot paper will look like this:

*Choose, in your own order of preference, six different persons from the approved list of candidates. To the candidate you most wish to see in government, you should allocate 6 points; to your next favourite, you should allocate 5; and so on. At the same time, you should consider in which post you want each to serve. Accordingly, you should write one name in each column, and one in each row.*

| | Your choice of names | | | | | |
|---|---|---|---|---|---|---|
| | 6pts | 5pts | 4pts | 3pts | 2pts | 1pt |
| Premier | | | | | | |
| Deputy PM | | | | | | |
| Min of Peace | | | | | | |
| Min of Health | | | | | | |
| Min of Tax | | | | | | |
| Min of Land | | | | | | |

Obviously, the list of candidates shall include every member of parliament or council, for that's why they're there; the only exceptions will be those who have already served a term or two.

(For details of the count, please see appendix 5.)

The result, the common consensus of our elected representatives, will be the six candidates with the most points, and each will serve in the post to which, in the consensus of those voting, he/she is most suited.

And they too will then work together.

It's worth pointing out that such a democratically elected executive would, in fact, be a form of power-sharing, all-party coalition, government of national unity, round-table co-operation or call it what we will, depending on whether we're Northern Irish, Bulgarian, Israeli or Russian. Some earlier examples of such didn't work too well... but that was partly due to the fact that many of their participants continued to believe in majoritarianism. Consensually elected forums (or any other for that matter) will be able to work well, if they do so in consensus.

### B(ii) Choosing their sub-committee

If such is to consist of a chairperson, a deputy, and, say, four ordinary members, we may assume that everyone attaches equal importance to the first-named posts. In which case, a modified matrix may be used, and the basic layout thereof is as shown:-

| Points | POST | Your choice of names |
|--------|------|----------------------|
| 6 | Chairperson | |
| 5 | Deputy Chair | |
| 4 | Ordinary member | |
| 3 | Ordinary member | |
| 2 | Ordinary member | |
| 1 | Ordinary member | |

I need hardly add that the candidate with the highest score will take the chair, the runner-up will be the deputy, and the next four also-rans will join as members. And these six will also work together... but there again, folks in cross-party sub-committees normally do.

There is one inherent disadvantage in the matrix vote and the modified matrix, and it is this: the voter need only choose a limited number as opposed to all of the candidates; so the bigot, if tempted, could doubtless opt for only his own. (And we're all bigots, to some extent anyway; I for one am an anti-nuke fanatic, and as for my views on majoritarianism... )

If the danger is real, perhaps the best approach is to vote in two stages, just as the electorate might if and when there are more than a dozen candidates (see page 22). Such a danger may be regarded as minimal, however, if the number of ministers to be elected is sufficiently high, i.e., greater than ten. Furthermore, it may well disappear altogether when the party system of politics is not the rigid set-up that it is to-day, both here and abroad. In such an ideal situation, people will appoint someone to a certain ministry on account of that person's suitability, and in the matrix vote experiment referred to in the dedication, the local Belfast councillor chosen to look after the health chair was, needless to say, a doctor, and whether he was God-fearing, and which God he feared, was apparently of little concern.

Sub-committees tend to be smaller, but as there are usually quite a few of them, the approved list of candidates for any one sub-committee will invariably be relatively small. Thus the bigot will run short of like-thinkers. Just in case, though, it may be wiser for everyone to choose all the subcommittee chairpersons in a matrix vote, and then to use modified matrices to choose their members.

The advantage of these two matrix voting systems is that they offer the voter the maximum amount of choice. Despite the one aforementioned limitation, therefore, their deployment is advisable, especially when all other decisions are also subject to some form of consensus voting.

The question as to which voting system shall be used on which occasion shall remain, as always, with the consensors. The politicians shall decide what to do and who shall do it; the consensors merely tell them how they will make these decisions.

In a consensual democracy, there may still be two ways of doing things: either we the people elect a legislature, and it then chooses its executive; or we elect, in two separate votes, first the one and then the other.

On balance, I think I prefer the former. The executive therein will consist of democratically elected folk, whereas separately elected presidents, be they Russian or American, have a nasty habit of appointing all sorts of non-elected "advisers". Secondly, what with their presidential councils and so on, these executives have tended to become mini-legislatures as well. Thirdly, we are no different from us, and we seem to elect the same sort of people no matter what the election. And lastly, the legislature's consensually elected executive will consist of a good number and, as we saw earlier, the greater that number, the greater the degree of fairness.

So if millions elect hundreds, and these hundreds then elect a score, proportionality will be maintained, and the government will represent all the people (and not just (less than) half of them).

# CHAPTER 7

# THE ELECTION CAMPAIGN

In both x-vote elections and in PR, there's a certain psychological thought process which basically works like this: *I* vote for what *I* want; I hope there'll be more of me and less of you, and you, well, by the sound of some of those campaign slogans, you can go to hell.

In effect, the x-vote almost forces us to be selfish; PR-STV allows us to be consensual if we want to be, but it still permits the dogmatic to be intransigent; the preferendum, however, asks us all to be consensual, as of right.

Now because the present systems are in effect orientated towards selfishness, all politicians are at least tempted to play on these emotions. Some exploit our feelings of greed, and we've all heard those promises and seen those pre-election budgets; others, even worse, exploit our fears. In Northern Ireland again, many an election campaign has been marked by heightened violence. In Britain, the Falklands (Malvinas) war led to a "khaki election". And in the United States, in nearly every post-war and pre-Gorbachev presidential election, the he (and sure, it was always a he) who was the more belligerent, was invariably the winner, and the American democratic system was actually a part of the arms race!

How frail we all are. How dominant the force of fear. Yet much is due to the simple fact that we resolve the fates of millions in for-or-against votes.

Candidates, naturally enough, are also frail. And it's easier for them, not to try and persuade us that they are absolutely right, rather to convince us their opponent is wrong. Hence many an election is littered with charge and counter-charge, and one accuses the other of being weak, an appeaser, and God knows what else besides. Hence again those nasty party slogans - defeat this, no to that, smash the other - it is all the language of war.

Everything takes on a negative air; and folks vote, not so much *for* a policy let alone a philosophy, more *against* a supposed opposite.

In consensus voting, though, as we said earlier, we all vote only for. What's more, as was noted on page 19, there's more to be gained in wooing an opponent. So an altogether different psychology is involved.

In a word, in a consensual democracy, *"Thou shalt not vote against thy neighbour."*

I still vote for my own candidate, of course, but I also recognise the candidature of your nominee, and I will give him/her at least 1 point, regardless, as was mentioned earlier, of his/her age, sex, colour, religious belief or, as may now be added, *political persuasion.*

Conciliation, then, is something we must all practice, not just in word (in talking), but also in deed (in voting).

In days to come, further evolution of our species may be possible. At the moment, however, many candidates are actually self-appointed, each deciding that he/she is right and all right if not in fact brilliant. Again, it seems, our democratic system suffers from a bias towards selfishness as these self-opinionated folk join in a win-or-lose struggle for political power.

Perhaps it would be better, therefore, if there were no candidates at all, or, to put it another way, if everyone was a candidate. In every constituency, folks could just choose, say, six names from amongst those there resident, and political position might come to be regarded more as a one-off duty, rather like jury service. If such was the case, maybe even the modest would get elected. In a consensual milieu, they wouldn't feel too far from home, as few would be struggling for power... not least because no one would get it.

The danger of such no-candidate or all-candidate elections is similar to that mentioned on page 27, namely, they allow the political, religious or nationalist bigot to be so. For the time being, therefore, maybe it's better to progress to the straightforward multi-candidate preferendum in which that same good bigot, if he's to be democratic in the full sense of the word, must cast some points for all. And we'll move on to the no-candidate system of elections, just as soon as we have a no-party system of democracy. Which is all in chapter 10.

# CHAPTER 8

# PROBABILITIES OF POWER

In one-party dictatorships, the probability of the dictator getting it all his own way is literally 1 in 1; that's obvious enough.

In two-party democracies, however, all is subject to the vote. And quite right too. But if, as is usually the case, the decision is based on a for-or-against vote, then the chances of any one political leader being able to dominate proceedings are, in theory, 1 in 2. If again, however, that leader has a majority in the house, then the whole damn thing is a foregone conclusion, and his chances of success are the same as those of he whose system he abhors, 1 in 1.

Thus, when it came to the crunch, Thatcher was able to steam-roller her poll tax through, just like a petty dictator. She is by no means the only leader so to act, neither in her own party, nor indeed in her own country.

Let us now see what the score will be in a consensual democracy, first in regard to a policy decision, then apropos an election.

## A   A Policy

If a certain matter is to be resolved in a six-option preferendum, the theoretical chances of any one leader getting most of what he wants are down to at least 1 in 6; if, furthermore, the issue is a contentious affair and if, therefore, there's a close-run vote, the consensors will be obliged to produce a composite result, and the chances of this hallowed politico having all his wishes fulfilled are probably down to 1 in 720, (see appendix 6). Which again suggests compositing is a good thing.

## B An Election

In electing its representatives, parliament may use a preferendum, a modified matrix or a matrix vote. The probabilities involved in each are as follows.

### i) The Preferendum

(If they elected just the one person in a six-candidate ballot, the chances of any one person being able to insist on his own point of view would again be just that, 1 in 6. However, as we said earlier, they should always elect more than one.)

So if they're electing two persons, a chair and a deputy, say, in the same six-candidate preferendum, the chances of any one particular set of results will be 1 in 15. (Please see appendix 6, pages 65-66.)

### ii) A Modified Matrix

If our representatives opt to elect a sub-committee of six members from a list of ten candidates using a modified matrix, such as is shown on page 26, the chances of any one leader getting his own chosen half-dozen will be 1 in 210, and if he wants his own personal choice of chair and deputy chair as well, his chances will be even smaller: 1 in 6,300. (For the sums involved, again, please see appendix 6, pages 67-68.)

### iii) The Matrix Vote

As the choice of each voter gets bigger, so too the chance of any one leader being able to dictate proceedings gets smaller and smaller. If they now elect a named six-member cabinet from the same ten candidates as per the matrix vote ballot paper shown on page 25, each will be able to vote in any one of 100,000,000 different ways. (See page 70.)

*Ipso facto*, the likelihood of any one person being able to win everything will be minimal:

- his chances of being able to insist, successfully, on his own chosen six will be as in the modified matrix, 1 in 210;
- if, in addition, he must have so-and-so as his premier, the odds go down to 1 in 1,260;
- if the old diehard demands his own deputy as well, they'll stand at 1 in 6,300;
- and if the bigot rants on about his own particular nominees for all six posts, it's down again to 1 in 151,200.

No matter which way you look at it, therefore, the chances of any one person being able to rule a consensual parliamentary roost will be greatly reduced. Consensus, in effect, spells the end for any personality cults, be they those of the one-party state, Stalin and his -ism, or those of the two-party systems, such as are seen in the very existence of words like thatcherism and reaganomics.

Believe it or no, consensus politics will actually allow our democratic institutions to do what they were designed to do in the first place. The legislature, by itself, shall make the decisions; and these shall be represented and/or executed by its chosen representatives in the executive. Hence the words.

Accordingly, the emphasis on leadership will be much reduced. The highest authority in the land will be the legislature; and the executive will be mere functionaries, either to implement parliament's decisions or, in natural and/or other emergencies, to be thoroughly accountable thereto.

In a consensual democracy, therefore, no matter what the decision, no one party or leader shall win everything; but everyone will win something. Whence our consensually elected representatives' consensually elected representatives, each so different perhaps one from another, will at last be able to (live and) work together, Bush with Jackson for example, male with female, Christian with Moslem and Hindu, each representing the consensual decisions of a parliament in which the interests of each and all are consensually represented.

# CHAPTER 9

# CONSENSUS – A HUMAN RIGHT

In days of old, the kings did say, their right to rule was divine. The bishops wise then blessed this belief... and everyone suffered as one righteous monarch fought another, each with the bishops' God supposedly on their side.

We now know that on (nearly) every occasion, both sides were wrong.

Eventually, of course, the sovereigns were persuaded (by various bloody means) to relinquish their power to the advocates of democracy. From henceforth, it was said, decisions would be taken in debate, and the minority would submit to the wishes of the majority. Compared to the previous order in which all were at the mercy of some mad monarch or crackpot dictator, this new majority rule was bound to be a great improvement.

And it was natural enough, I suppose, for all to think in terms of for-or-against votes, for was not everything either true or false, of God or of the devil, with the forces of good or those of evil? Furthermore, did we not have the two arms, and could we not exercise righteous judgement by raising the right one?

So for-or-against it was to be, with all or most decisions based on a two-option vote; thus the words 'majority' and 'minority' entered the political lexicon... and many societies as a result split into two.

If but to justify its own position, the bigger "half" concocted the so-called right to majority rule. Sometimes, the smaller "half" agreed, for it too hoped to form a majority, come the next election.

In other societies where the powerless never reached the 50% threshold, either because their numbers were too small (as with the nationalists in

Northern Ireland) or because of the voting system (as in South Africa), alienation set in. But such was and is a feature of the traditional two-party state as well, for there too the majority often rides roughshod over the interests of the minority; and in supporting this very system of majority rule, the latter itself also rides roughshod over any smaller minorities. Hence in Britain, for instance, the demise of the Liberals in the '60s, and the current failure of the Greens.

So might I suggest that majoritarianism is as badly wrong as the divine royal right which preceded it.

I suppose there's little wrong in a simple for-or-against vote, if all concerned agree to its use. The question, "Shall we now break for lunch?" may very easily be resolved by a straight show of hands. If, however, the issue is more serious, and if, therefore, the minority should refuse to accept such a majority decision, then that majority shall have no right whatsoever to insist on the enactment thereof. (Nor, for that matter, shall the minority have the right to a total veto.) Thatcher, to return to the poll tax example, may have had a majority (in the House); but she had no consensus for that policy, neither in the House nor in the country, and therefore she had no right whatsoever to force it through.

As a democratic tool, then, the for-or-against vote is hopelessly inadequate. It either leads to division in lands otherwise united, or it exacerbates the tensions in split communities. It might have been OK, for a time; it was, in its day, a big improvement; but it has served its historical purpose and it must now be replaced by something better.

For everyone has the right to participate in government. We all deserve to be heard. Democracy is for everybody, not just 50% and a bit. And consensus is a human right.

Now to divide into two opposing camps may have seemed natural; but maybe it's even more natural for folks to come together. The most obvious (pro)creative power is inherent in a union of male and female, but there is also an amazing potential to be gained if, for instance, the Western materialist could but learn from the Eastern mystic. And a real peace will emerge, be it in Northern Ireland or in the world at large, with a "coming together of our opposites".

Thus may we conclude that there was no divine right of kings, and that there is no right to majority rule. Indeed, in any serious dispute, the very use of the simple majority vote may be an infringement of that minority's human rights.

A true democracy should reflect in its legislation the average opinion of all its citizens; everyone has the right to influence that average opinion in equal measure; so maybe consensus voting is right too.

We might even suggest the following clause be added to the UN declaration:-

*"No decision shall be passed into law, unless it enjoys a level of consensual support of at least, (say), 75%."*

# CHAPTER 10

# CONSENSUS
# AND THE SURVIVAL OF OUR SPECIES

The politics of consensus, I'd like to suggest, are directly related to the reform of three aspects of human behaviour which cannot be allowed to continue unchanged.

Firstly, we know the world will not survive unless we stop fighting wars. We must, therefore, resolve all future conflicts peacefully.

This simply cannot be done with a majority vote. Indeed, in Northern Ireland, Nagorny Karabakh, Kosovo and elsewhere, a belief in majoritarianism is actually a part of the problem. One side wants majority rule within *these* borders, the other within *those*...

But as we saw in the last chapter, neither has the right to rule its corresponding minority without taking the latter's interests into account. Secondly, to greater or lesser extent, all national borders are artificial concoctions of the human mind anyway. Thirdly, we all have a responsibility towards our neighbours. So on all three counts, yet again, both sides are wrong.

And maybe, its unwise, even to take sides.

The solution to any conflict will always involve a degree of compromise; to achieve a solution, therefore, we must first employ a decision making process in which compromise options will also be considered.

So in theory, no matter what or where the conflict, the use of a preferendum, preceded if necessary by a parliamentary debate or public inquiry in which all reasonable views may be aired, could both facilitate, and be a part of, the reconciliation process. It is, if you like, the very catalyst of consensus.

Secondly, the world will not survive if we fail to tackle our mounting ecological crises.

Within a majoritarian system, any government in power tends to see everything in terms of win-or-lose, and the most important item on its agenda is probably the winning of the next election. Hence the short term tax concessions, immediate exploitation of a few more resources, and so on. In a word, the future is often sacrificed for the sake of the present, and a majoritarian form of democracy may actually be a threat to the survival of this planet.

What's more, no majority of West European and American petrol consumers has the right to ignore the wishes of a minority, the Pacific Islanders, for example. To solve such problems as global warming, we really must co-operate.

Thirdly, the world will not survive if we fail to evolve. Just as the world progressed from the monarchies of yesterday to the mainly majoritarian democracies of to-day, so must we now move on to a more pluralistic multi-party or even no-party democracy.

The kings, alas, were reluctant to change; to persuade our present day leaders of the advantages of consensus may be just as difficult. Hopefully, however, all will be achieved in a much more peaceful manner...

...for the very existence of the computer makes such a reform inevitable, a natural consequence of the use of multi-option voting. The party system evolved from, and still depends on, the simple for-or-against vote. If everything's a case of *this* or *that*, all too easily will the *this* whip demand that all *this* -party members vote for *this,* because who on earth would vote for *that*? When, however, all is subject to a six-option preferendum, say, and when therefore it's a question of 720 *"thises and thats"*, the whips will be rendered redundant. In other words, consensus voting will lead to a break-up of the present two-party political system.

Parties may still exist, of course, parties, groups, lobbies and organisations. But they will be free associations, and the formal party power structures we know at present will inevitably fade.

What's more, such an evolutionary step forward will in itself promote further evolution. In the present majoritarian forms of government, those inspired by a new idea have to air their views, promote them, round up support... and they'll only get their idea adopted once it gets the backing of a majority. If science worked under the same principles, poor old Einstein would still be preaching the proofs of relativity.

Take, for example, the case of PR-STV, first mooted in Britain over a hundred years ago, and still nowhere to be seen on that island (except in its church's synod).

In consensus politics, however, any new idea will as it were immediately affect the common consensus, just as a baby child will affect the national average height, the moment it's born. If, what's more, it's a good idea and survives the test of time, it will gradually become more popular and, albeit slowly, be incorporated into the system of government.

Consensus, then, is evolutionary, in both senses of the word, an important part of our brave new world...

But it' s needed now, for otherwise we may not get there.

# CHAPTER 11

# NIRVANA

We are all neighbours on this planet, and in accepting the need to live in sympathy with our environment, we should first seek a reconciliation in the human one.

We must, therefore, live, talk and vote *with* each other, each as I say acknowledging the validity of others' aspirations and/or candidatures.

Thus, to return once more to Northern Ireland, the extreme unionist/nationalist must give at least 1 point to those of an opposite persuasion. In so doing, he/she shall recognise that some are better than others... and the inherent psychological effect of each having to accept literally everyone as a neighbour may make an incalculable contribution towards a mutual understanding and accommodation. (So too, methinks, will the results of such elections!)

In like manner, the Azerbaijanis will vote, not only for their fellow Azerbaijanis, but also for their fellow Armenians; the Sunnis will vote for the Shi'ites, the Israelis for the Palestinians, the Albanians for the Serbians, every individual starting this reconciliation process... with him/herself.

In conventional politics, too, the socialist will vote with the capitalist, and both with the ecologist; the rich will vote with the poor, and both will profit thereby. And so it goes on.

Consensus, if you like, suggests a certain pacifism, a pacifism of the mind. I'm certainly not going to back up my proposal by military force; but nor will I insist on same by virtue of its numerical support. I simply ask for the right to air it, and for you to consider it; for the right to participate in government

And just as violence breeds violence, so will consensus encourage yet further consensus.

But the greatest benefit may well be this: when all our political elders first seek and then find their common consensus, and when every conflict is resolved in a quiet and civilised manner, the effect on society in general and especially on the young...

...oh who can know? The full consequences of consensus cannot be predicted. Suffice to say we'll be one step nearer the omega.

# APPENDICES

## APPENDIX 1

## A Preferendum

## THE CONSTITUTIONAL FUTURE OF NORTHERN IRELAND

*Write a 10 opposite the option you like the most; write a 9 opposite the option you think is second best; write an 8 opposite your third choice; and so on, to the end, whence you should write a 1 opposite the option you like least of all. Your vote will be valid if, and only if, you complete the ballot paper, (in your own order of choice), from 10 to 1.*

| OPTION | Points |
|---|---|
| A  Northern Ireland to be integrated into the United Kingdom | |
| B  Northern Ireland to part of a unitary state Republic of Ireland | |
| C  Northern Ireland to be devolved within the United Kingdom | |
| D  Northern Ireland to be in a 2-part federation with the Republic of Ireland | |
| E  Northern Ireland to be a 9-county unit in a 4-part federation with the ancient Provinces of Ireland | |
| F  Northern Ireland to be part of an Anglo-Celtic Federation | |
| G  Northern Ireland to be administered by both Britain and Ireland within a strengthened Anglo-Irish agreement | |
| H  Northern Ireland to be an independent statelet | |
| I  Northern Ireland to be under direct rule from London, with no Anglo-Irish agreement | |
| J  Northern Ireland to be administered as at present, the Anglo-Irish agreement unchanged | |

## APPENDIX 2

### Maxima and Minima

## A. The Preferendum

In all analyses, the consensors should be aware of the relevant theoretical levels which any one option or candidate might achieve.

The maximum possible level of consensus is always 100% of course, but the minimum is never zero; such, by definition, would be a total abstention. A minimum, then, is a whole load of 1s, so our minima and average levels vary according to the following table:-

| In a | | | |
|---|---|---|---|
| **3**- option/candidate preferendum the minimum level of consensus is | **33%**, the average | **67%** |
| **4**- option/candidate preferendum the minimum level of consensus is | **25%**, the average | **63%** |
| **5**- option/candidate preferendum the minimum level of consensus is | **20%**, the average | **60%** |
| **6**- option/candidate preferendum the minimum level of consensus is | **17%**, the average | **58%** |
| **7**- option/candidate preferendum the minimum level of consensus is | **14%**, the average | **57%** |
| **8**- option/candidate preferendum the minimum level of consensus is | **13%**, the average | **56%** |
| **9**- option/candidate preferendum the minimum level of consensus is | **11%**, the average | **55%** |
| **10**-option/candidate preferendum the minimum level of consensus is | **10%**, the average | **55%** |

or, just to keep the mathematician happy, the maximum, minimum and average levels of consensus are:

$$100\%, \qquad \frac{100\%}{N} \qquad \text{and} \qquad \frac{100 \times (N+1)\%}{2N} \qquad \text{respectively;}$$

where N is the number of options/candidates.

## B. The modified matrix and the matrix vote.

In these elections, the result is an entire sub-committee or a complete executive. If V is the valid vote in an election of X persons from a list of N candidates, then the maximum and minimum scores of any one candidate will be (X x V) and 0 respectively. Our main concern, however, relates to L, the level of consensus of the overall result, and this is given by the following formula:

$$L = \left\{ \frac{\text{total number of points cast for all winning candidates}}{\text{total number of points cast for all candidates}} \right\} \times 100\%$$

Thus the maximum level of consensus, 100%, would be achieved if all those voting only chose the successful ones.

## APPENDIX 3

### The Preferendum Count

On many occasions, the count will be done on a computer. It can, however, be done by hand, and to show how it all happens, I've chosen a simple five-option/candidate preferendum, in which just the three of us - you, I and another - take part.

You, let us say, vote
like this:

| | |
|---|---|
| A | 1 |
| B | 5 |
| C | 4 |
| D | 2 |
| E | 3 |

My opinion is:

| | |
|---|---|
| A | 3 |
| B | 4 |
| C | 5 |
| D | 2 |
| E | 1 |

And another says:

| | |
|---|---|
| A | 1 |
| B | 3 |
| C | 4 |
| D | 2 |
| E | 5 |

Let us now record your vote. On a computer panel (or piece of paper) it would look like this:

| OPTION or CANDIDATE | THE VOTES | | | | |
|---|---|---|---|---|---|
| | 5pts | 4pts | 3pts | 2pts | 1pt |
| A | | | | | 1 |
| B | 1 | | | | |
| C | | 1 | | | |
| D | | | | 1 | |
| E | | | 1 | | |

We may note at this stage that you exercised all your preferences, and you voted for all the options/candidates. Thus the above completed picture shows a 1 in each column and a 1 in each row.

Now we'll record my vote as well, adding it to yours:

| OPTION or CANDIDATE | THE VOTES | | | | |
|---|---|---|---|---|---|
| | 5pts | 4pts | 3pts | 2pts | 1pt |
| A | | | 1 | | 1 |
| B | 1 | 1 | | | |
| C | 1 | 1 | | | |
| D | | | | 2 | |
| E | | | 1 | | 1 |

and finally, we'll add another's:

| OPTION or CANDIDATE | THE VOTES | | | | |
|---|---|---|---|---|---|
| | 5pts | 4pts | 3pts | 2pts | 1pt |
| A | | | 1 | | 2 |
| B | 1 | 1 | 1 | | |
| C | 1 | 2 | | | |
| D | | | | 3 | |
| E | 1 | | 1 | | 1 |

So far, so good. On a completed count of three votes, every column should add up to 3, as too should every row. If one of them doesn't, then either the vote was invalid, or we recorded it incorrectly... and if such is the case, the computer will bleep bleep.

Let us now press another button, so to get the points. These we will add up to give five separate totals, each of which we will then express as a percentage of the maximum possible score (in this case, 15), so to get five levels of consensus. Thus a second panel would look like this:

| OPTION or CANDIDATE | THE POINTS | | | | | TOTALS | LEVELS OF CONSENSUS |
|---|---|---|---|---|---|---|---|
| | 5pts | 4pts | 3pts | 2pts | 1pt | | |
| A | | | 3 | | 2 | 5 | 33% |
| B | 5 | 4 | 3 | | | 12 | 80% |
| C | 5 | 8 | | | | 13 | 87% |
| D | | | | 6 | | 6 | 40% |
| E | 5 | | 3 | | 1 | 9 | 60% |

Agáin, each column adds up, and any mistake would be readily apparent.

The result is obvious enough, perhaps, but may I now refer you back to chapter 4.

In just such a five-option preferendum, each voter casts a total of: $5 + 4 + 3 + 2 + 1 = 15$ points, and this the mathematician describes as $\Sigma 5$.

In an N-option/candidate preferendum, then, each casts a total of $\Sigma N$ points, and if V is the valid vote, the final count can be verified (by the computer) according to the following bottom line:

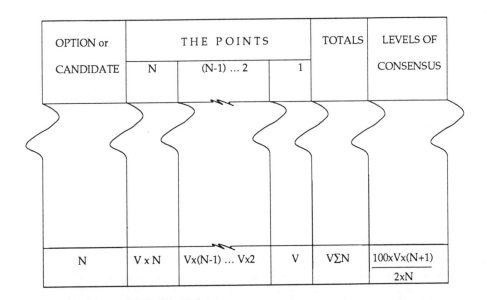

| OPTION or CANDIDATE | THE POINTS | | | TOTALS | LEVELS OF CONSENSUS |
|---|---|---|---|---|---|
| | N | (N-1) ... 2 | 1 | | |
| N | V x N | Vx(N-1) ... Vx2 | V | V$\Sigma$N | $\dfrac{100 \times V \times (N+1)}{2 \times N}$ |

Finally, we may wish to put all of the above into a formula, for such may be required by the computer programmer:

If, in an N-option/candidate preferendum,

the number of Npts votes cast for option A is $A_N$

the number of (N-1)pts votes cast for option/candidate A is $A_{(N-1)}$

and so on, and if V is the valid vote, then $L_A$, the level of consensus obtained by option A, shall be given by the following formula:

$$L = \left\{ \frac{A_N \times N + A_{(N-1)} \times (N-1) + \ldots + A_2 \times 2 + A_1}{V} \right\} \times 100\%$$

## APPENDIX 4

### *A Preferendum Analysis*

The following two examples, both rather hypothetical perhaps, show what might happen in the preferendum analyses of two contentious debates or elections.   We'll first have a look at a little five-option/candidate ballot, and then at a more complicated ten-option vote.

If but for the sake of simplicity, let us assume that 100 people voted, each casting his/her preference points as he or she might wish.  And let's say that, as it so happens, 55 individuals gave 5 points to A, 10 gave 5 points to B, and that the entire picture of how everybody voted looks like this:

| OPTION or CANDIDATE | THE VOTES | | | | |
|---|---|---|---|---|---|
| | 5pts | 4pts | 3pts | 2pts | 1pt |
| A | 55 | | | | 45 |
| B | 10 | 20 | 40 | 20 | 10 |
| C | 20 | 20 | 20 | 20 | 20 |
| D | | 10 | 20 | 50 | 20 |
| E | 15 | 50 | 20 | 10 | 5 |

So if we now press that second button to get the points totals, we'll get the following display:

| Option or | THE POINTS | | | | | TOT | Levels |
|---|---|---|---|---|---|---|---|
| Candidate | 5pts | 4pts | 3pts | 2pts | 1pt | | of cons |
| A | 275 | | | | 45 | 320 | 64% |
| B | 50 | 80 | 120 | 40 | 10 | 300 | 60% |
| C | 100 | 80 | 60 | 40 | 20 | 300 | 60% |
| D | | 40 | 60 | 100 | 20 | 220 | 44% |
| E | 75 | 200 | 60 | 20 | 5 | 360 | 72% |

Well, option/candidate A is obviously seen as very divisive and aconsensual; B and C are viewed with little enthusiasm; D is regarded as a very poor suggestion; but E enjoys some consensual support, it seems, and sure enough, E gets the highest score: 72%.

If the preferendum concerns a policy issue, the consensors will now form up a composite result based on option E, enriched if possible by any commensurate aspects of option A, perhaps by B and C though that's unlikely, and perhaps again by the negation of D.

If on the other hand it's an election of, say, two persons, then E and A will be the chosen two.

For our second example, we'll take a ten-option vote. The panel displays are therefore a little more complex, but the logic is the same.

First, then, the votes:

| OPTION or CANDIDATE | THE VOTES | | | | | | | | | |
|---|---|---|---|---|---|---|---|---|---|---|
| | 10 pts | 9pts | 8pts | 7pts | 6pts | 5pts | 4pts | 3pts | 2pts | 1pt |
| A | 30 | 20 | 10 | | | | | 5 | 15 | 20 |
| B | 20 | 15 | 5 | | | | | 10 | 20 | 30 |
| C | 20 | 10 | 10 | 5 | 5 | 5 | 5 | 10 | 10 | 20 |
| D | 20 | 15 | 15 | 10 | 10 | 5 | | 5 | 10 | 10 |
| E | 10 | 10 | 10 | 10 | 10 | 10 | 10 | 10 | 10 | 10 |
| F | | 30 | 20 | 20 | 10 | 10 | 10 | | | |
| G | | | 20 | 40 | 30 | 10 | | | | |
| H | | | 10 | 15 | 25 | 25 | 15 | 10 | | |
| I | | | | | 10 | 10 | 20 | 25 | 25 | 10 |
| J | | | | | | 25 | 40 | 25 | 10 | |

And then the points:

| OPTION or CANDIDATE | THE POINTS | | | | | | | | | | TOT | LEVELS OF CONS. |
|---|---|---|---|---|---|---|---|---|---|---|---|---|
| | 10pts | 9pts | 8pts | 7pts | 6pts | 5pts | 4pts | 3pts | 2pts | 1pt | | |
| A | 300 | 180 | 80 | | | | | 15 | 30 | 20 | 625 | 62.5% |
| B | 200 | 135 | 40 | | | | | 30 | 40 | 30 | 475 | 47.5% |
| C | 200 | 90 | 80 | 35 | 30 | 25 | 20 | 30 | 20 | 20 | 550 | 55.0% |
| D | 200 | 135 | 120 | 70 | 60 | 25 | | 15 | 20 | 10 | 655 | 65.5% |
| E | 100 | 90 | 80 | 70 | 60 | 50 | 40 | 30 | 20 | 10 | 550 | 55.0% |
| F | | 270 | 160 | 140 | 60 | 50 | 40 | | | | 720 | 72.0% |
| G | | | 160 | 280 | 180 | 50 | | | | | 670 | 67.0% |
| H | | | 80 | 105 | 150 | 125 | 60 | 30 | | | 550 | 55.0% |
| I | | | | | 60 | 50 | 80 | 75 | 50 | 10 | 325 | 32.5% |
| J | | | | | | 125 | 160 | 75 | 20 | | 380 | 38.0% |

On a close inspection of the above, we see that options/candidates A and B are both regarded as being very extreme; C is felt to be less extreme perhaps, but still rather divisive; and D, though slightly more popular, is still somewhat aconsensual. E, meanwhile, seems bland indeed. H, if we may jump a little, appears a bit empty, while I and J are viewed with scepticism if not scorn. But now, returning to F, we see that though it gets no 10s at all, it nevertheless gets a very good score; and even G, with no 9s or 10s to its name, is still seen as a good compromise.

We may note in passing that C, E and H all get an exact mean level of consensus. The reason is simple, for all three received symmetrical voting patterns, so no wonder their totals are average. This would be even more apparent if we drew the relevant histograms.

Again, the consensors must interpret these results. Any policy decision will be a composite based on F as enhanced by G definitely, and D perhaps, etc.. While any election of, say, three representatives would see F, G and D elected, in that order.

Now if, as in this example, option F is indeed combined with option G, (that or candidates F and G are both declared elected), with levels of consensus $L_f$ and $L_g$ respectively, then the new overall level of consensus, $L_{fg}$, may be determined by the following formula:

$$L_{fg} = L_f + (100 - L_f)\% \times L_g$$

If, furthermore, option D is also incorporated (or if candidate D also gets elected), then this new overall level, $L_{fgd}$, shall be given by:

$$L_{fgd} = L_{fg} + (100 - L_{fg})\% \times L_d$$

## APPENDIX 5

### *The Matrix Count*

In appendix 3, we were able to calculate the common consensus of just the three of us - thee, me and another - using a preferendum. Now, in similar style, we'll have a go at a matrix vote, so to find what is our common consensus on who should serve in a government of six from our parliament of ten.

The ballot paper we'll use is the example shown on page 25. So, after seriously considering all the candidates, you let us say decided to fill in your voting slip as follows:

| | Your choice of names | | | | | |
|---|---|---|---|---|---|---|
| | 6pts | 5pts | 4pts | 3pts | 2pts | 1pt |
| Premier | | | Sam | | | |
| Deputy PM | | | | | | Bob |
| Min of Peace | Jo | | | | | |
| Min of Health | | Pat | | | | |
| Min of Tax | | | | | Ann | |
| Min of Land | | | | Tom | | |

Any casual observer could thus conclude you're absolutely committed to peace, and Jo, you feel, is the best one for that job. Health is also one of your priorities, while the post of Deputy PM, in these days of consensus, is of little concern to you. In all, there's a lot of information to be gleaned from an examination of your completed ballot, but that's because you had a lot of choice.

You, of course, are different.  I, old hack that I am, voted in a more traditional way:

|  | My choice of names | | | | | |
|---|---|---|---|---|---|---|
|  | 6pts | 5pts | 4pts | 3pts | 2pts | 1pt |
| Premier | Fred | | | | | |
| Deputy PM | | Bob | | | | |
| Min of Peace | | | | | Sam | |
| Min of Health | | | | | | Jo |
| Min of Tax | | | | Ann | | |
| Min of Land | | | Sean | | | |

While another had this to say:

|  | Another's choice of names | | | | | |
|---|---|---|---|---|---|---|
|  | 6pts | 5pts | 4pts | 3pts | 2pts | 1pt |
| Premier | Jo | | | | | |
| Deputy PM | | | | Sam | | |
| Min of Peace | | | | | Tom | |
| Min of Health | | Pat | | | | |
| Min of Tax | | | Mary | | | |
| Min of Land | | | | | | Paul |

If we now list all ten candidates and table the points received by each, we get the following display:

| | Candidates | | | | | | | | | | Relative |
|---|---|---|---|---|---|---|---|---|---|---|---|
| | Jo | Fred | Pat | Bob | Sam | Sean | Mary | Tom | Ann | Paul | Importance |
| Premier | 6 | 6 | | | 4 | | | | | | 16 |
| Deputy PM | | | | 5+1 | 3 | | | | | | 9 |
| Min of Peace | 6 | | | | 2 | | | 2 | | | 10 |
| Min of Health | 1 | | 5+5 | | | | | | | | 11 |
| Min of Tax | | | | | | | 4 | | 3+2 | | 9 |
| Min of Land | | | | | | 4 | | 3 | | 1 | 8 |
| TOTALS | 13 | 6 | 10 | 6 | 9 | 4 | 4 | 5 | 5 | 1 | |

By looking at the bottom row of individual totals, we can see who are our six most popular candidates: Jo, Pat, Sam, Fred, Bill, and either Tom, or Ann. They shall form the government, so say the three of us.

Next, by examining the right hand column, we can see the degree of importance we attach to each post. The above matrix may thus be simplified into the following display, and please note the re-arranged order:

| | Candidates | | | | | | | | Relative |
|---|---|---|---|---|---|---|---|---|---|
| | Jo | Pat | Sam | Fred | Bob | Tom | Ann | Other | Import |
| Premier | (6) | | 4 | 6 | | | | | 16 |
| Min of Health | 1 | (10) | | | | | | | 11 |
| Min of Peace | 6 | | (2) | | | 2 | | | 10 |
| Deputy PM | | | 3 | | (6) | | | | 9 |
| Min of Tax | | | | | | (5) | 4 | | 9 |
| Min of Land | | | | | | 3 | | 5 | 8 |
| TOTALS | 13 | 10 | 9 | 6 | 6 | 5 | 5 | 9 | 63 |

Now by looking at this matrix, we can see in which ministerial post each successful candidate should serve. We simply take the highest individual scores (some of which are shown bracketed, 10 and 6, for instance), and thus appoint the person indicated to the ministerial post indicated. In the event of a tie, priority is given first to the person with the higher total, and then to the more important post. In the above example, the consensors would thus reason according to the following logic:

The highest individual score is Pat's 10 for health, so she gets that job. Then, of the four 6s, the most popular person in the most popular post puts Jo in the premiership, and that rules out her second 6 for the peace post, as well as Fred's 6 for the premiership. Bob's 6 for deputy still stands, however. Next comes Ann's 5 for tax which puts paid to Tom's ambitions; (never mind, he was obviously one of the less popular figures in parliament, and he was only contending a minor post; all the tensions of a majoritarian vote play a much reduced part in any consensual contest). Finally, to allocate the last two, Sam with a 2 goes to peace, so Fred with nothing goes to land.

Thus may we now draw up the following matrix, the result of all our deliberations, our tripartite consensus. (And even if three hundred of us had voted, the final picture would be just about as simple.)

|  | Candidates | | | | | | | Relative |
| --- | --- | --- | --- | --- | --- | --- | --- | --- |
|  | Jo | Pat | Sam | Fred | Bob | Ann | Other | Importance |
| Premier | 6 | | | | | | | 1*b* |
| Min of Health | | 10 | | | | | | 11 |
| Min of Peace | | | 2 | | | | | 10 |
| Deputy PM | | | | 6 | | | | 9 |
| Min of Tax | | | | | 5 | | | 9 |
| Min of Land | | | | 0 | | | | 8 |
| TOTALS | 13 | 10 | 9 | 6 | 6 | 5 | 14 | 63 |

Of all the 63 points cast, 49 of them were used to get the six successful candidates elected; this corresponds to a level of consensus of 77%. Secondly, if we add up the above individual scores in the matrix, 29, we may ascertain how many of the points actually served their intended purpose.

We could, if you like, do a more detailed analysis. For of the 49 points cast in favour of the chosen six, 18 were yours, 17 mine and 14 another's. Secondly, of the successful 29 points in the individual matrix scores, 8 were yours, 10 mine and 10 another's. Each, then, gets roughly a third, and if you lose a little on the consensual swing, you'll gain a *soupçon* on the roundabouts.

In general, therefore, it's fair to say that both the preferendum and the matrix vote are highly proportional, and maybe more so than any other system of humble human origins.

## APPENDIX 6

### *Freedom of Choice versus Abuse of Power*

## A. The Preferendum

(In a 2-option/candidate referendum, there's a choice of only 2 possible opinions, and that's that)

| In a | | |
|---|---|---|
| 3- option/candidate preferendum, there's a choice of | 6 | possible opinions and/or emphases |
| 4- option/candidate preferendum, there's a choice of | 24 | possible opinions and/or emphases |
| 5- option/candidate preferendum, there's a choice of | 120 | possible opinions and/or emphases |
| 6- option/candidate preferendum, there's a choice of | 720 | possible opinions and/or emphases |
| 7- option/candidate preferendum, there's a choice of | 5,040 | possible opinions and/or emphases |
| 8- option/candidate preferendum, there's a choice of | 40,320 | possible opinions and/or emphases |
| 9- option/candidate preferendum, there's a choice of | 362,880 | possible opinions and/or emphases |
| 10- option/candidate preferendum, there's a choice of | 3,628,800 | possible opinions and/or emphases |

or, as the mathematician would say, in an N-option preferendum, the total number of opinions and/or emphases which may be expressed is:

$$N \times (N-1) \times (N-2) \times ... \times 2 \times 1.$$

This is known as factorial N, and written as N!

Now as we suggested on page 32, greater choice for us, the voters, and/or for them, our elected representatives, means less opportunity for any one leader to dominate. Thus, in a simple N-option preferendum in which they're aiming to choose just the one simple policy, the theoretical chances of any such leader being able to dictate proceedings will be at least 1 in N; in practice, especially when compositing is involved, they're more likely to be 1 in N!.

Similarly, if we or they are electing a fixed number of persons, (X), from a choice of N candidates, or maybe they are selecting X items from a "shopping list" of N possibles, each (and let's say she's a she) may choose any one of N persons or items as her first choice, any one of (N-1) as her second choice, and so on, and this she does X times. In other words, each will have a choice of:

$$N \times (N\text{-}1) \times (N\text{-}2)x \ldots\ldots \times [N\text{-}(X\text{-}1)] \quad = \quad \frac{N!}{(N\text{-}X)!}$$

different ways of voting. If the order in which these X persons or items are elected is of no particular importance - and needless to say, there are X! different orders in which X objects can be selected - then the probability of any one particular set of X being chosen will be:

1 in $\dfrac{N!}{X! \times (N\text{-}X)!}$   where N > X, and X > 1

*(formula A)*

If, however, the order of elections does matter, the probability of any one particular order will be:

1 in $\dfrac{N!}{(N\text{-}X)!}$

*(formula B)*

Thus, if we refer to the example given on page 33, namely, a preferendum election for two representatives from a list of six candidates, each of our elected representatives will have a choice of 720 different ways of voting, and so the chances of any one party leader or whoever being able to insist on only his own proposals will be:

$$1 \text{ in } \frac{6!}{2! \times (6-2)!}$$

$$= \quad 1 \text{ in } \frac{6!}{2! \times 4!}$$

$$= \quad 1 \text{ in } \frac{6 \times 5}{2}$$

$$= \quad 1 \text{ in } 15.$$

If, however, he's saying that old so-and-so must be the chair, and whatshisname the deputy, his chances will be found by using formula B:

$$1 \text{ in } \frac{6!}{(6-2)!}$$

$$= \quad 1 \text{ in } \frac{6!}{4!}$$

$$= \quad 1 \text{ in } 6 \times 5$$

$$= \quad 1 \text{ in } 30.$$

## B. The Modified Matrix

If they now choose a sub-committee of X persons from a ballot paper of N candidates, and if, again, it matters not in which order they are elected, an ambitious leader's chances of getting his own nominees chosen will be as above in the preferendum:

$$1 \text{ in } \frac{N!}{X! \times (N-X)!}$$

*(formula A)*

When the order of election does matter, the odds get tighter. So if the old tyrant wants to insist on a certain number (Y) of named office bearers within this sub-committee, (whence X > Y), then the likelihood of his total success will be:

$$1 \text{ in } \frac{N!}{(X-Y)! \times (N-X)!}$$

*(formula C)*

And if he's really intransigent and seeks to nominate not just Y but all X persons, and in his own particular order, his chances will be smaller still:

$$1 \text{ in } \frac{N!}{(N-X)!}$$

*(formula B)*

Thus, in the particular modified matrix of ten candidates mentioned on page 33, the chances of the despot getting his own chosen six may be ascertained using formula A:

$$1 \text{ in } \frac{10! \times 6!}{6! \times (10\text{-}6)!}$$

$$= \quad 1 \text{ in } \frac{10 \times 9 \times 8 \times 7}{4 \times 3 \times 2}$$

$$= \quad 1 \text{ in } 210.$$

Similarly, his chances of getting not only his four ordinary members (in any order of election), but his two named office bearers as well, will be found according to formula C:

$$1 \text{ in } \frac{10!}{(6\text{-}2)! \times (10\text{-}6)!}$$

$$= \quad 1 \text{ in } \frac{10!}{4! \times 4!}$$

$$= \quad 1 \text{ in } \frac{10 \times 9 \times 8 \times 7 \times 6 \times 5}{4 \times 3 \times 2}$$

$$= \quad 1 \text{ in } 6,300$$

Lastly, his chances of getting all his own six members elected in his own particular order will be given according to formula B:

$$1 \text{ in } \frac{10!}{4!}$$

$$= \quad 1 \text{ in } 10 \times 9 \times 8 \times 7 \times 6 \times 5$$

$$= \quad 1 \text{ in } 151,200.$$

## C. The Matrix Vote

If our elected representatives are now to elect an executive of X members from a list of N candidates using a matrix vote, the choice involved will be very large indeed. Each - this one's a he - may choose any one of N candidates for any one of X posts, so his first choice is one of (NxX). For his second selection, he has a choice of (N-1) candidates for any one of (X-1) posts, that is, any one of {(N-1) x (X-1)} possibilities. And so on, X times. In theory, then, the total number of different ways of voting

$$\frac{N! \times X!}{(N-X)!} \qquad \text{where again, } N > X.$$

*(formula D)*

So the chances of any abuse may be absolutely infinitesimal.

Let's take the example shown in appendix 5, an executive of six ministers chosen from a list of ten candidates. In such a matrix vote, the total number of different ways of voting will be given by this formula D:

$$\frac{10! \times 6!}{(10\text{-}6)!}$$

$$= \quad \frac{10! \times 6!}{4!}$$

$$= \quad 10! \times 6 \times 5$$

$$= \quad 10 \times 9 \times 8 \times 7 \times 6 \times 5 \times 4 \times 3 \times 2 \times 6 \times 5$$

$$= \quad 100,000,000$$

And that's just a simple example! If we now take the British House of Commons, and if let's say 635 MPs were to choose a government of 21 ministers in a matrix vote, each would be able to choose any one of those 635 members to serve in any one of these 21 ministerial posts, then any one of 634 to serve in any one of 20, and so on. In all, every MP would be able to vote in any one of $2.6 \times 10^{78}$ different ways, give or take a squared million or so.

It's all a great advance on 2.

As a general rule, it's always better to cater for the maximum possible freedom of choice. Just as, yesterday, any increase of power in a parliament worked to reduce the power of the monarch, so too, to-day, any additional choice acquired by our representatives will serve to reduce the power of the party leaders. There can be little to fear in that.

Leaders, or those who aspire to be such, will be with us for a long time yet, I suppose. We must therefore ensure that the chances of these people ever becoming a Stalin or a Hitler are very much reduced, (and it's sobering to recall that while the first emerged in a one-party state, the second succeeded from within a multi-party system).

As I've tried to demonstrate, consensus voting can be just such a guarantee. I should add, however, that the above odds are maxima, and they take no account of what happens if, prior to the vote, the aspiring despot tries to bribe, threaten or whip (to use the term still in British parliamentary parlance) the elected representatives to vote, not as they might wish to, but as he dictates.

There again, if our collective conscious is ready for the politics of consensus, we have little to fear, and everything to hope for.

# INDEX

* for definitions of these terms, please see page x.